Cultural Celebrations

BON FESTIVAL

by Elizabeth Andrews

DiscoverRoo
An Imprint of Pop!
popbooksonline.com

WELCOME TO DiscoverRoo!

This book is filled with videos, puzzles, games, and more! Scan the QR codes* while you read, or visit the website below to make this book pop.

popbooksonline.com/bon

abdobooks.com

Published by Pop!, a division of ABDO, PO Box 398166, Minneapolis, Minnesota 55439. Copyright © 2024 by Abdo Consulting Group, Inc. International copyrights reserved in all countries. No part of this book may be reproduced in any form without written permission from the publisher. DiscoverRoo™ is a trademark and logo of Pop!.

Printed in the United States of America, North Mankato, Minnesota.

102023
012024

Cover Photo: Getty Images, Shutterstock Images

Interior Photos: Getty Images, Shutterstock Images, Wikimedia Commons, 2020 Kyodo News/AP Images

Editor: Emily Dreher
Series Designer: Colleen McLaren

Library of Congress Control Number: 2023938823

Publisher's Cataloging-in-Publication Data

Names: Andrews, Elizabeth, author.
Title: Bon festival / by Elizabeth Andrews
Description: Minneapolis, Minnesota : Pop!, 2024 | Series: Cultural celebrations | Includes online resources and index
Identifiers: ISBN 9781098245344 (lib. bdg.) | ISBN 9781098245900 (ebook)
Subjects: LCSH: Bon Festival (Buddhist festival)--Juvenile literature. | Ullambana--Juvenile literature. | All Souls' Day (Buddhism)--Juvenile literature. | Holidays--Juvenile literature. | Cultural sociology--Juvenile literature.
Classification: DDC 394.26--dc23

*Scanning QR codes requires a web-enabled smart device with a QR code reader app and a camera.

TABLE OF CONTENTS

CHAPTER 1
Dances and Drums 4

CHAPTER 2
History of Bon 8

CHAPTER 3
Welcoming Spirits 14

CHAPTER 4
Celebrate!. 22

Making Connections. 30
Glossary 31
Index. 32
Online Resources 32

CHAPTER 1
DANCES AND DRUMS

Haruko has been busy spending time with her family. All her older cousins are visiting from the city. They're staying at her house for the next few days. It's the Bon festival!

WATCH A VIDEO HERE!

The Bon festival is a good time to catch up with friends and family.

Haruko's cousins have been practicing their drums. They even showed her how to play some beats. It's the second day of Bon, so festivities in town begin. Haruko's cousins are performing on the taiko drums. Her mom and aunts will be dancing. Haruko is most excited for the street food!

Okonomiyaki *is a grilled Japanese pancake.*

Taiko drummers are powerful, energetic performers.

The Bon festival in Japan is also called Obon. It is one of the three major holiday seasons in the country. Bon is a time to **honor** and celebrate ancestors and their spirits. It is believed that the spirits of the dead revisit their living relatives. The first Japanese Bon took place in 606 CE.

CHAPTER 2
HISTORY OF BON

Bon traditions began in India. A **disciple** of Buddha spoke to the spirit of his dead mother. Her **soul** hadn't gone to a happy place. To help her, the disciple made **offerings** to Buddhist monks. After that, his mother's spirit was released from the bad place.

LEARN MORE HERE!

The fan dance is one of Japan's oldest dances.

DID YOU KNOW? Bon spread from India through China and to Japan.

The original ancient Japanese Bon holiday resembled the Buddhist All Souls Day. Both holidays honor the dead. Many Japanese people do not follow a specific religion. Most participate

The Bon holiday came to Japan when the Buddhist religion spread from India.

in ancestral **worship**. During Bon Festival, Japanese families clean their ancestors' graves, make offerings to **temples**, and light lanterns.

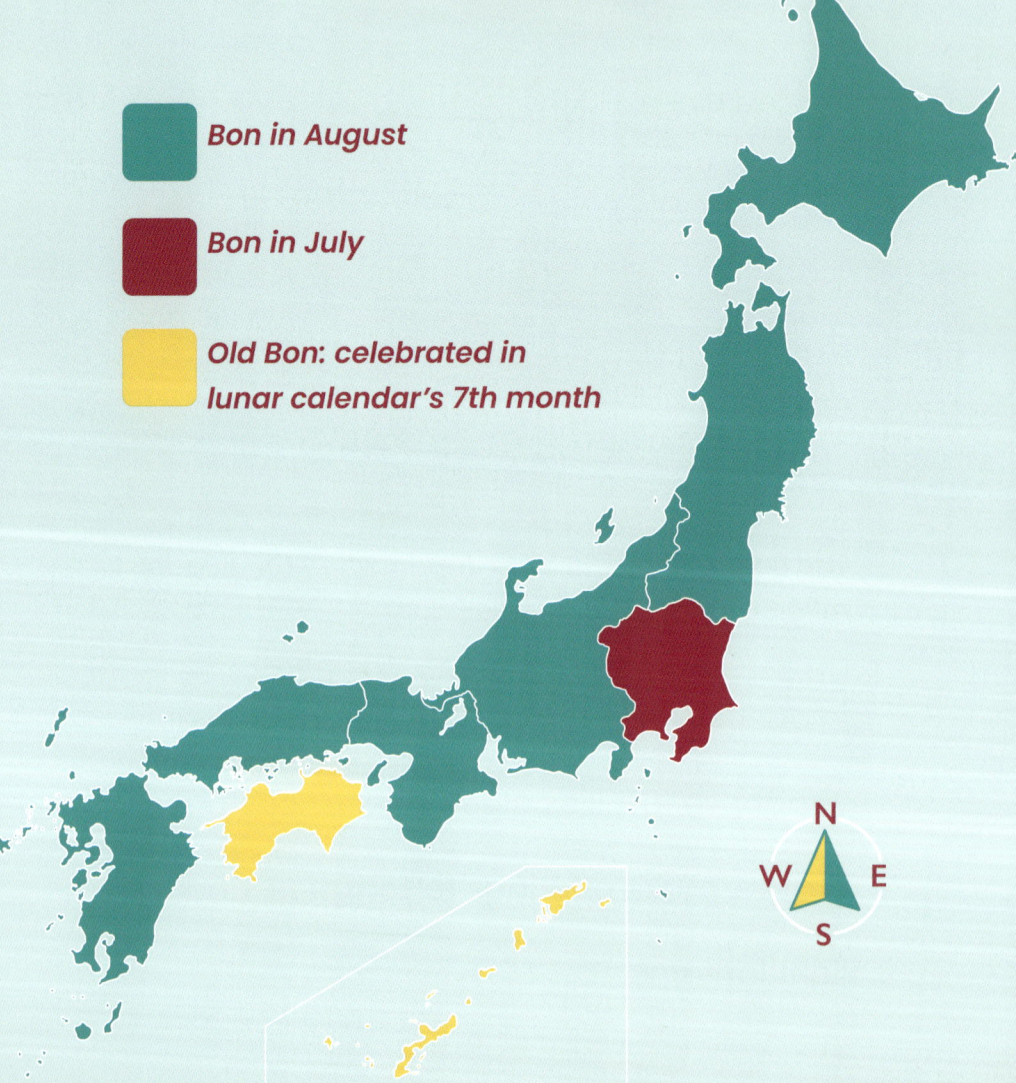

Bon falls on different dates around Japan. Shichigatsu Bon, meaning Bon in July, is celebrated from the 13th to the 15th of July. These dates follow the solar calendar that most of the world uses. Hachigatsu Bon (Bon in August) is celebrated the 13th to the 15th of August. Each region of Japan celebrates Bon in its own special way.

LUNAR CALENDAR

The lunar calendar follows the monthly cycles of the moon. A month begins with a new moon and has a full moon on day 15. It is about 29 ½ days to the next new moon. Lunar months have 29 or 30 days. There are 12 or 13 months in a lunar year. Adding an extra month every few years helps the lunar calendar line up with the traditional solar calendar.

Japan is the largest island country in East Asia.

CHAPTER 3
WELCOMING SPIRITS

During Bon, people welcome the spirits of dead family members back to their homes. Family is important in Japanese culture. In the past, homes were often **multigenerational**. Children could live in the same home as their parents, grandparents, and even great-grandparents.

EXPLORE LINKS HERE!

DID YOU KNOW? In the last 50 years, more people began leaving their family homes and living on their own once they reached adulthood.

In Japan, family names come first and given names come second.

There are more chances to be outside in rural Japan.

Bon lasts three days. Most businesses close so people can go home to celebrate. Since the festival **honors** spirits as they return to their birthplaces, people return to their family home. Many people leave big Japanese cities like Tokyo and Osaka for **rural** locations.

On the first day of Bon, the spirits of ancestors come home. Families clean gravesites. Fires and lanterns are lit to guide loved ones back home. The fires are called *mukaebi*. Families might go pray at **temples**. They will share special meals together.

Many Bon lanterns are made from paper.

The cucumber represents a fast horse that souls travel home on. The eggplant is a cow souls leave on.

Offerings are an important part of the Bon festival. Offerings have a **spiritual** meaning and are things such as food, flowers, and incense.

People bring their offerings to temples or gravesites. Some families may create **altars** in their homes. The offerings are made to connect the spirits of the dead with the living.

Gravestones are often decorated with incense, flowers, water, candles, and food.

In Kyoto, Bon ends with five giant fires lit on mountainsides. Each fire is a character or a shape with special meaning.

When it's time for people to say goodbye to their ancestors' spirits on the last day of Bon, farewell fires are lit on mountains. Families may also light floating lanterns and release them on rivers. This ceremony is called *Toro Nagashi*.

Floating lanterns are often lit and sent down rivers to say goodbye to spirits.

CHAPTER 4
CELEBRATE!

During the Bon festival, communities gather to dance and play music. Bon Odori is a type of folk dance. People of all ages dance together in the streets or at parks. Some dancers will dress in traditional Japanese clothing called *yukata*.

COMPLETE AN ACTIVITY HERE!

Yukata are clothes similar to kimonos but made of lighter cotton fabric.

The dances often show special things about the regions they are performed in. The local dances may have movements that look like a person is digging or

Awa Odori in Tokushima is the most famous Bon dance party.

Hanagasa Odori is performed with straws hats that have been decorated with flowers.

throwing nets for fishing. The dances tell parts of the region's history. Dancers sometimes use props such as fans, colorful towels, and wooden clappers.

Music is just as important as dancing during Bon. Traditional folk music is played on drums, string instruments, and bamboo flutes. There is also often a person calling out the words of the song. Usually, musicians play on a bandstand tower in the middle of the festival. Dancers move around it. Like Bon Odori, the music tells stories about each region and its history.

Traditional folk music is usually passed down through families.

DID YOU KNOW? Japanese people call the bandstand a *yagura*.

There is a lot of work to do before street festivals start.

As time has passed since the first Bon festival, people have stopped taking part in all the traditions. But it is still a special time to go back to the family home and remember loved ones who have passed.

Japanese children are taught to respect the spirits who come home to visit during Bon.

MAKING CONNECTIONS

TEXT-TO-SELF

What Bon tradition did you find most interesting? Please explain your answer.

TEXT-TO-TEXT

Have you read any books about holidays that honor family members who have passed on? If so, how were they similar to or different from Bon?

TEXT-TO-WORLD

Bon Odori dances tell the history of Japanese regions. What are other ways people present the history of places? How do you like to learn about history?

GLOSSARY

altar — a table or place that serves as a center of worship.

disciple — one who believes and spreads the teachings of another.

honor — to show respect.

multigenerational — consisting of more than one age group of family members.

offering — something given as a form of worship.

rural — of or relating to open land away from towns and cities.

soul — a nonmaterial part of a living being.

spiritual — having to do with religious matters or people's beliefs in things such as the soul or what happens after death.

temple — a building for religious worship.

worship — love, respect, and affection shown to an object, person, or being.

INDEX

altars, 19

ancestors, 7, 11, 17, 20

calendars, 12, 13

clothes, 22

dance, 6, 22–26

drums, 6, 26

family, 4, 6, 11, 14, 16–17, 19, 21, 29

fires, 17, 20

food, 6, 17, 19

Japan, 7, 12, 13, 16

lanterns, 11, 17, 21

music, 22, 26

offerings, 8, 11, 18–19

regions, 12, 13, 16, 24–26

temples, 11, 17, 19

DiscoverRoo! ONLINE RESOURCES

This book is filled with videos, puzzles, games, and more! Scan the QR codes* while you read, or visit the website below to make this book pop.

popbooksonline.com/bon

*Scanning QR codes requires a web-enabled smart device with a QR code reader app and a camera.